GEORGE PRICE'S
Characters

More than 200 of His
Best Cartoons

1955

SIMON AND SCHUSTER

NEW YORK

FIRST PRINTING
LIBRARY OF CONGRESS CATALOG CARD NUMBER: 55-10042
MANUFACTURED IN THE UNITED STATES OF AMERICA
PRINTED BY MURRAY PRINTING COMPANY, WAKEFIELD, MASS.
BOUND BY AMERICAN BOOK-STRATFORD PRESS, INC., NEW YORK

"It isn't me the gypsy's in. The gypsy's in Ed."

"They're not nearly as typical as I expected."

"I'll be glad when this crime wave is over. John isn't getting enough sleep."

"Wipe your feet!"

"What makes you think
being busy would make me happy?"

"You're kidding."

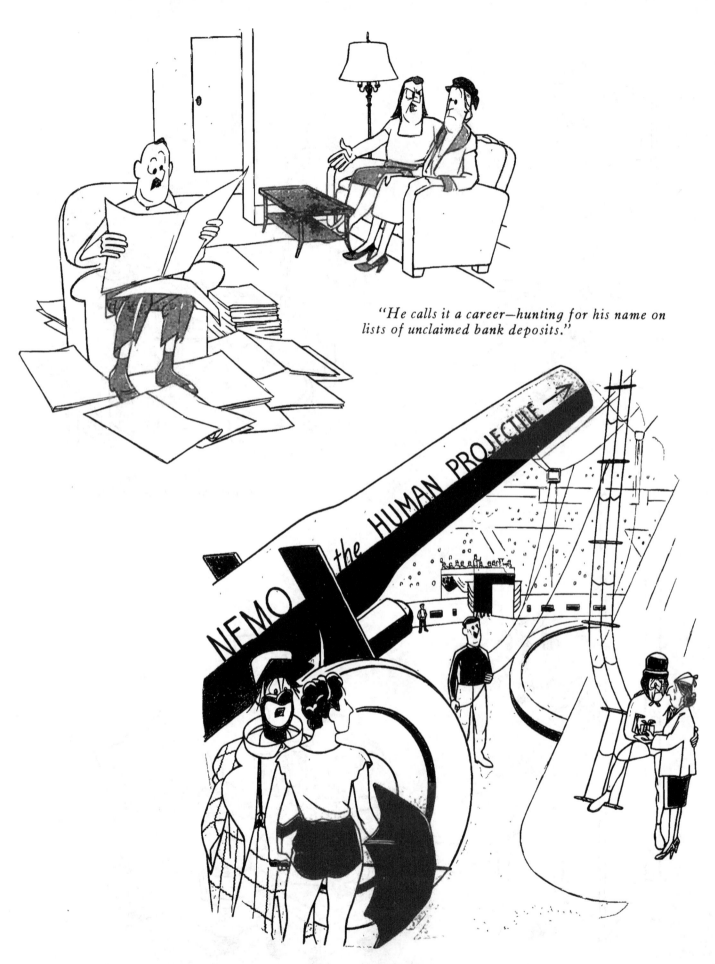

"He calls it a career—hunting for his name on lists of unclaimed bank deposits."

"It's very touching. Every time his act goes on, she's right there with a little going-away present."

"Grab a mitt. The world situation won't deteriorate any faster because you get in a little one o' cat."

"*Who asked you to share my interests?*"

"*Human beings only, damn it! Human beings only!*"

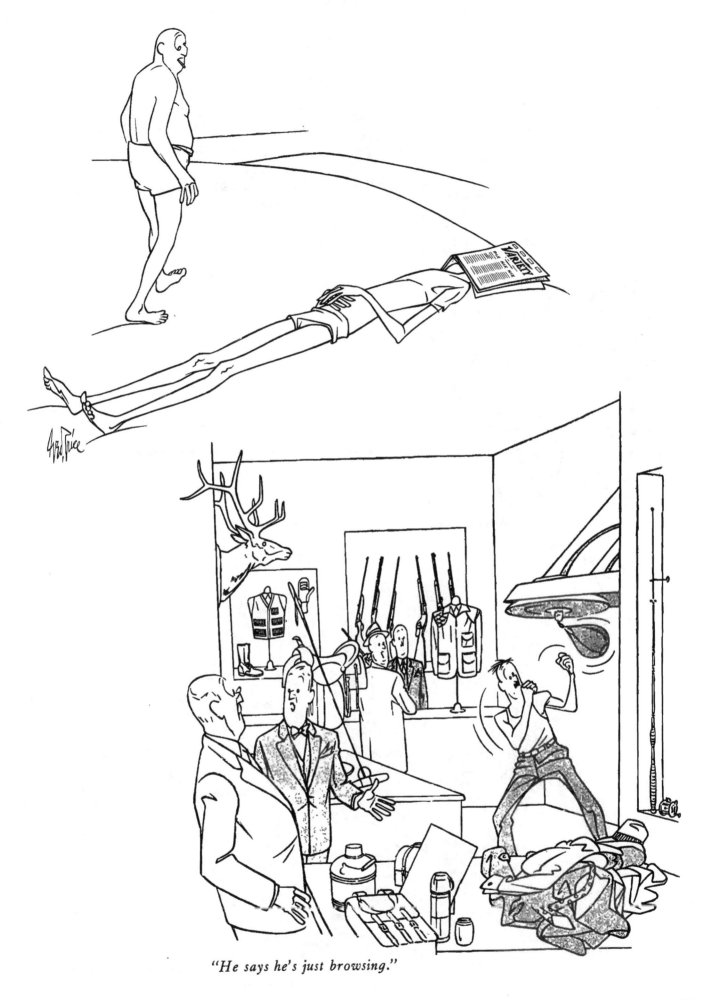

"He says he's just browsing."

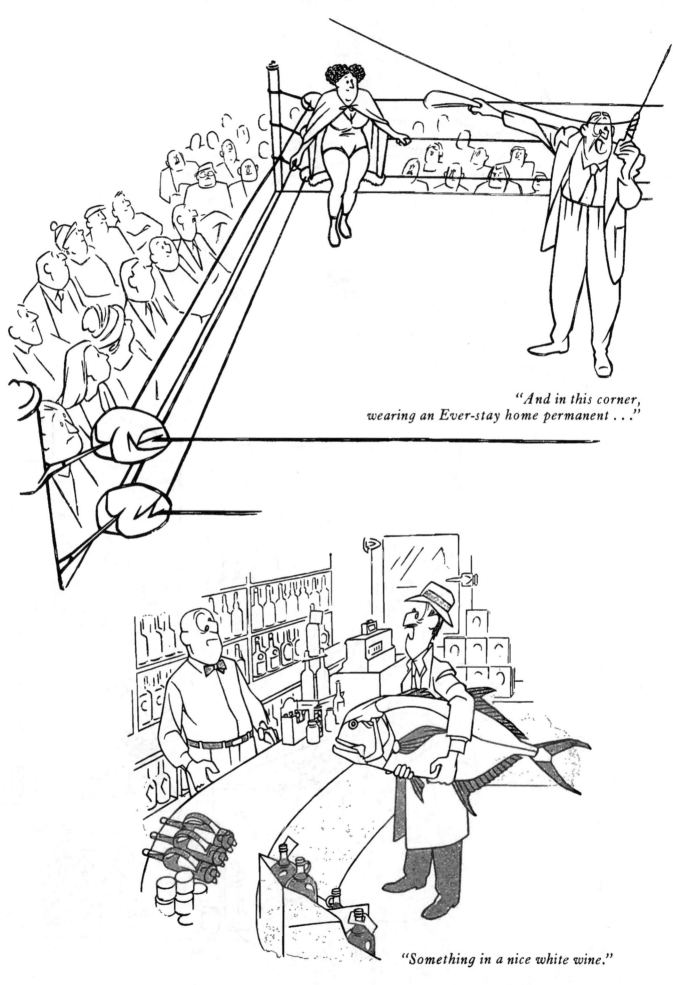

"And in this corner,
wearing an Ever-stay home permanent ..."

"Something in a nice white wine."

"Would you mind acting as
though you had just stumbled on uranium?"

"How does that feel—a little tight?"

"*Very good.*
Now without the glasses."

"I hate to make an issue of it.
He says he's left-handed and that's that."

"Carmichael, I'd like a word with you."

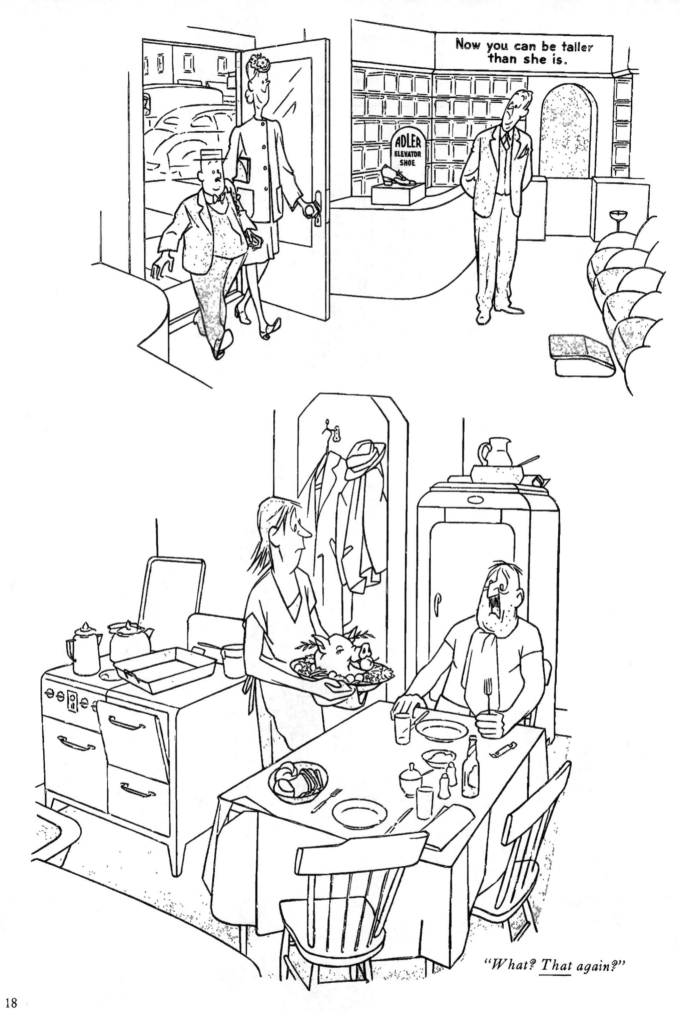

Now you can be taller than she is.

"What? <u>That</u> again?"

"*Mac makes a great thing out of these reconciliations.*"

"*Lord, what a day!*"

"Er—haven't you got one that's more resigned to its fate, so to speak?"

*"We had a cozy little package here until the
union demanded stand-ins."*

"Madam, it might interest you to know that you're competing with
the man who ran the fastest 220 in the Monongahela Valley Track Meet of 1928."

"Either find yourself a fence or lay off for a while. This clutter is driving me nuts."

"I was just about to give up on it when I got this idea that there might be a market for an automatic shuffler that doesn't shuffle."

"It's in excellent condition. The former owner was a psychoanalyst with a very small practice."

"I think he's had enough."

"...and what's more, you probably never will find an ad requesting intelligent companionship for an elderly millionaire."

"*Would you prefer Mendelssohn's 'Wedding March' or 'Lohengrin'?*"

*"I'm not listening to any
radio program. I'm listening to my wife!"*

*"That's the story men.
Now get out there and sell freezers."*

Don't fall for it. It's what they call psychology."

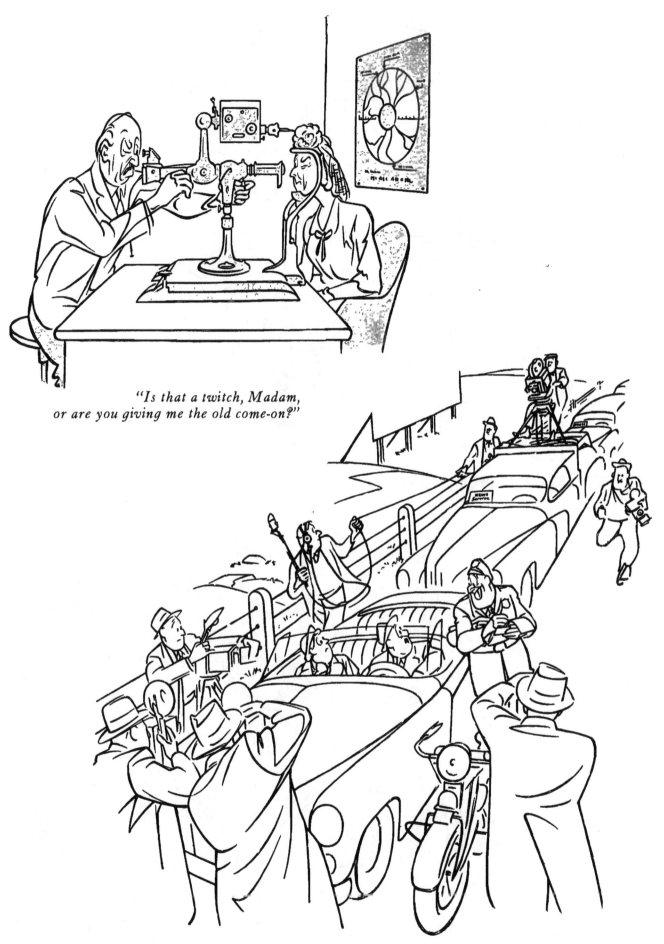

"Is that a twitch, Madam,
or are you giving me the old come-on?"

"Hope you folks don't mind. This happens to be my ten-thousandth arrest."

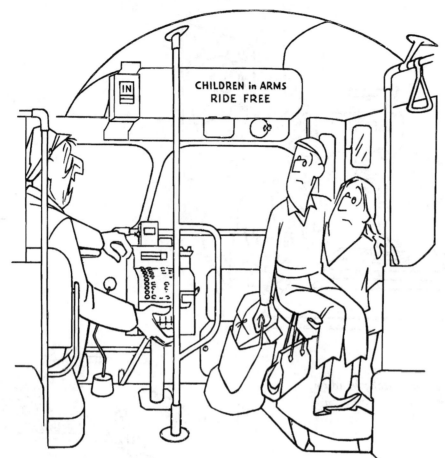

"Now look, lady, I've had a tough day."

"Would you care for some music to read by?"

"Truman it does something for. You it doesn't."

"Well, so far so good, Mrs. Madison."

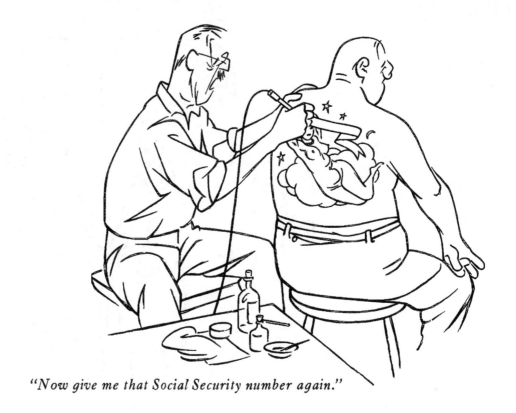

"Now give me that Social Security number again."

"I'm willing to say the hell with it if you are."

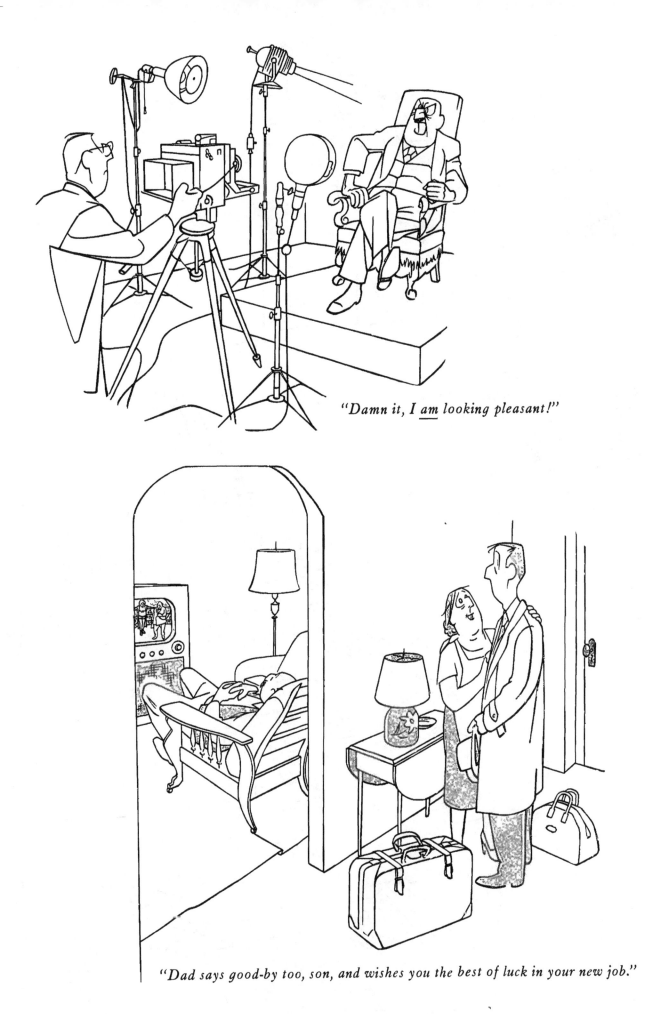

"Damn it, I _am_ looking pleasant!"

"Dad says good-by too, son, and wishes you the best of luck in your new job."

"I'm a boy."

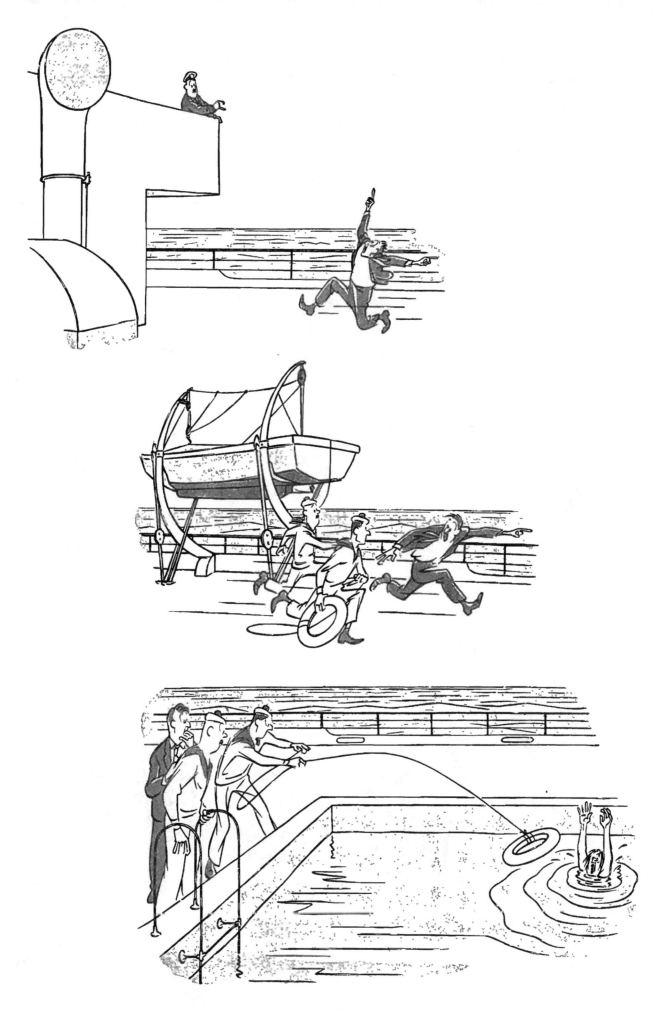

"Sam's Credit Clothing—212 Delancey Street—high quality—low prices—easy terms—"

"You mean he does it with just bread crumbs?"

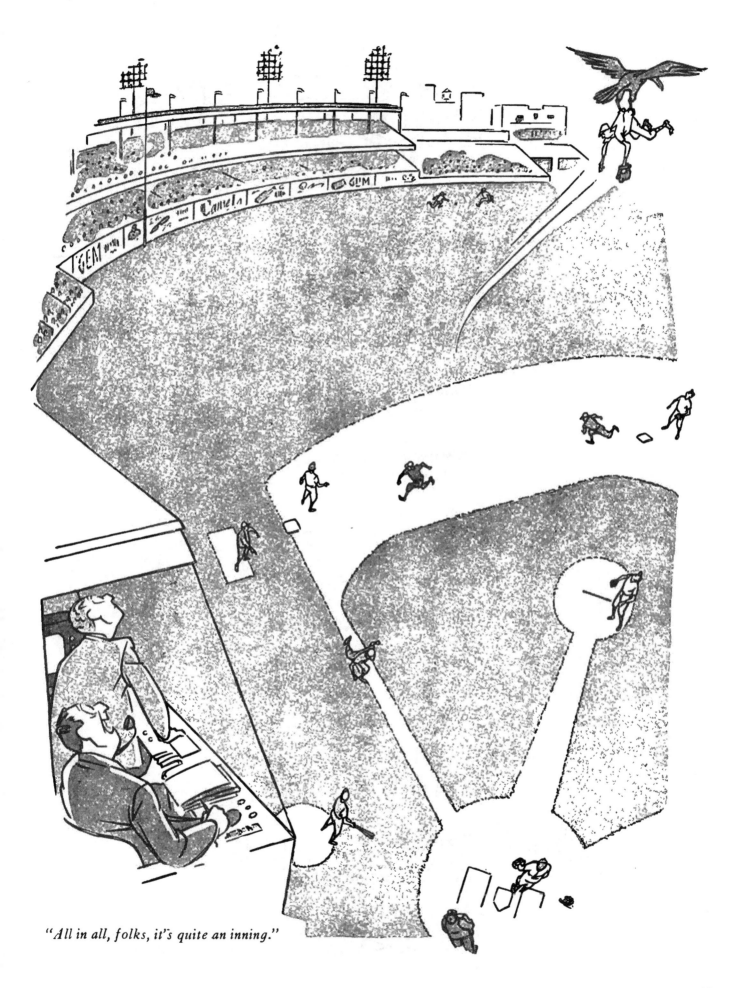

"All in all, folks, it's quite an inning."

"Well, maybe you're sitting
on the wrong end."

"They all say 'For Perfect Attendance—
Ridgewood First Parish Sunday School.'"

"Now don't hesitate to interrupt me for any important news bulletins."

"It's 'What?' 'Eh?' and 'How's that?' around here till I'm almost nuts."

"All right, Joe, you can knock off."

"*You can relax. There's a warm front moving up from Texas.*"

"*I'll say this for Harry. He's a good provider, he doesn't run around, and he's never struck me except in self-defense.*"

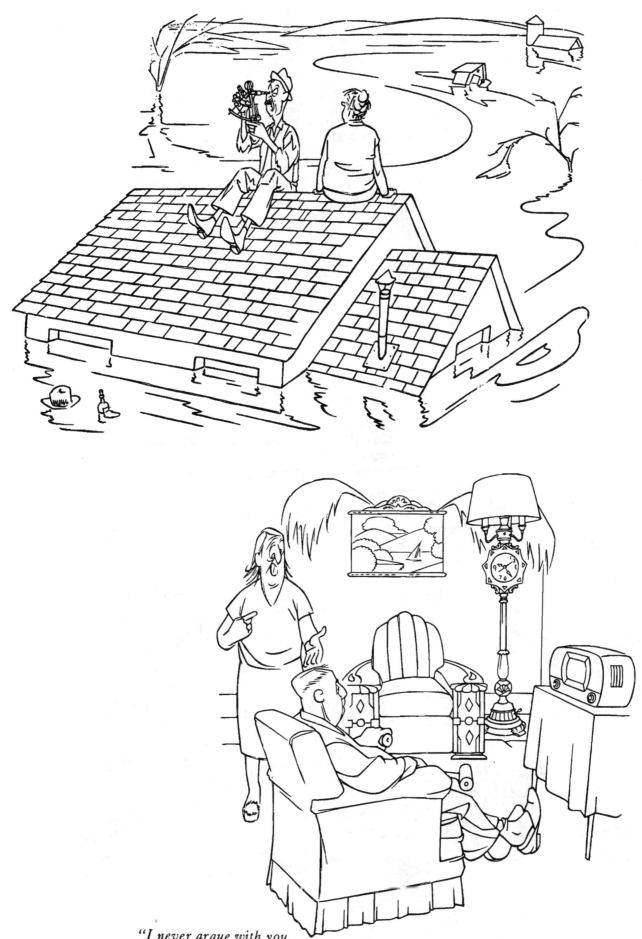

"I never argue with you
when you're right, so why always argue with me when I'm right."

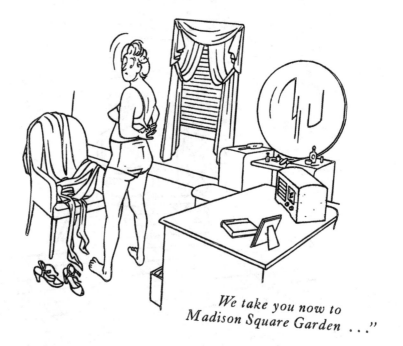

We take you now to Madison Square Garden . . ."

"Do you mind if I join you?"

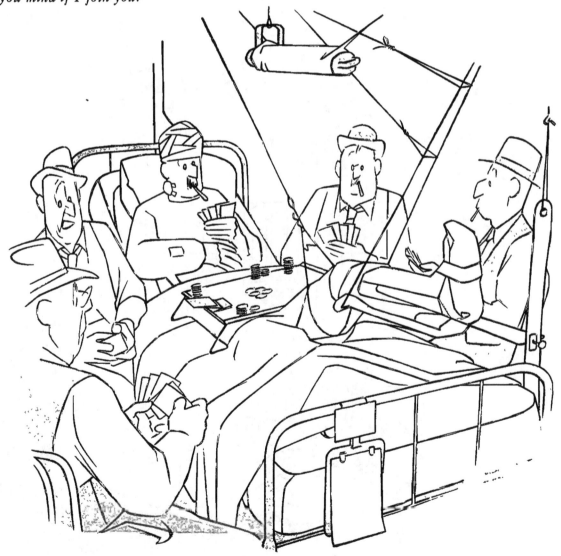

"My wife is skeptical, too."

"Hmm. Eighth Avenue, eh, and preferably in the Fifties?"

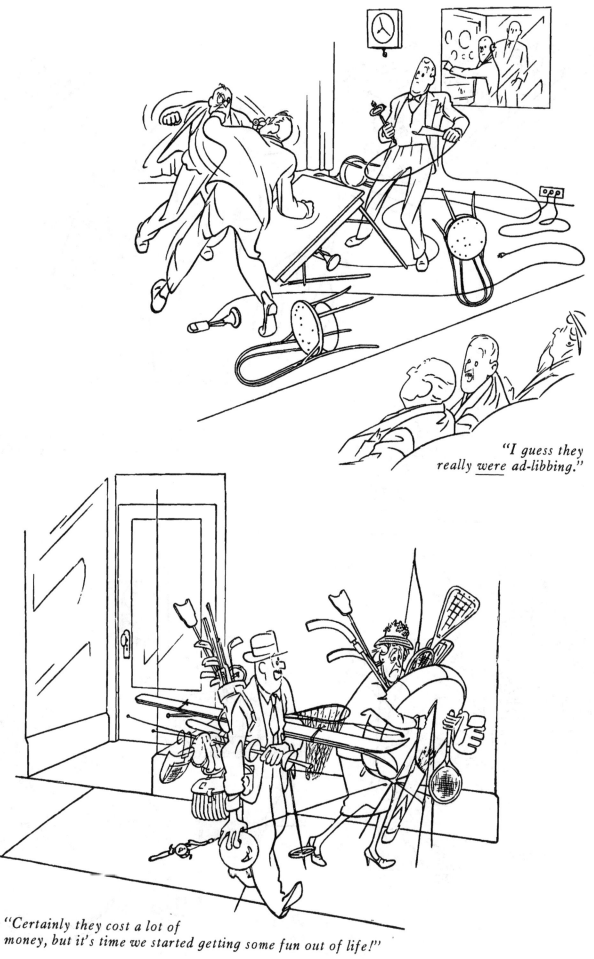

"I guess they really _were_ ad-libbing."

"Certainly they cost a lot of money, but it's time we started getting some fun out of life!"

"*Just drive straight ahead, sir.
We'll have you out of here in a jiffy.*"

"Cross my palm with silver."

"Twelve, please!"

"Madame must remember that
everybody doesn't see three sides of her at once."

"Watch out, Fred! Here it comes again!"

"It's poor Mr. Worthington. I understand his wife left him."

*"Very pretty, sir—but the Federal
Housing Administration can hardly advance money on an air castle."*

*"When I think of some of the men I might be
married to now if it hadn't been for you and that damn ukulele!"*

*"After you get perpetual motion
licked, you might take a crack at this leaky faucet!"*

"And now a word from my sponsor."

"Er—
might I have a hamburger?"

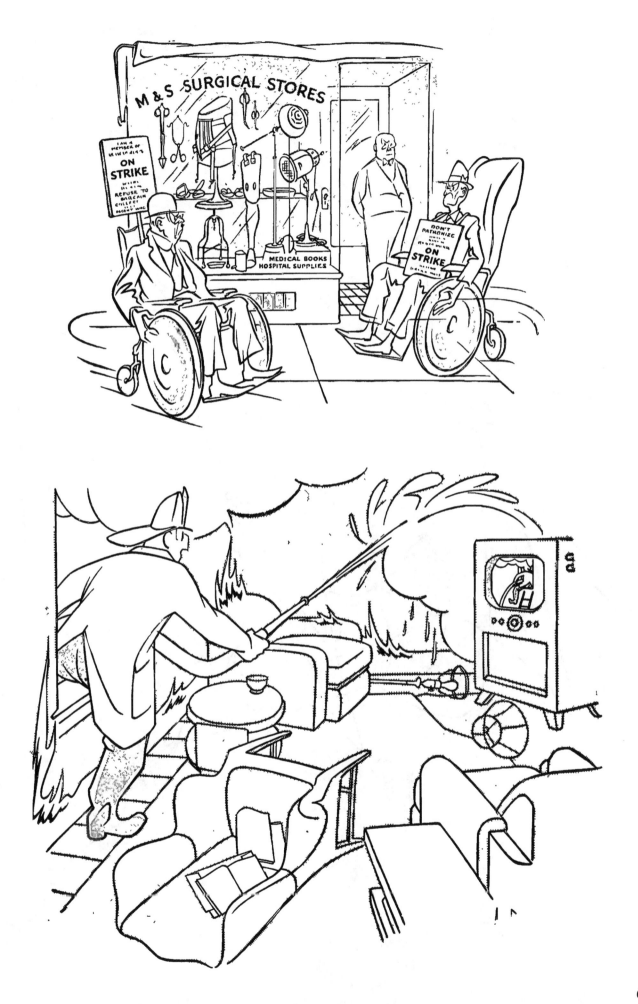

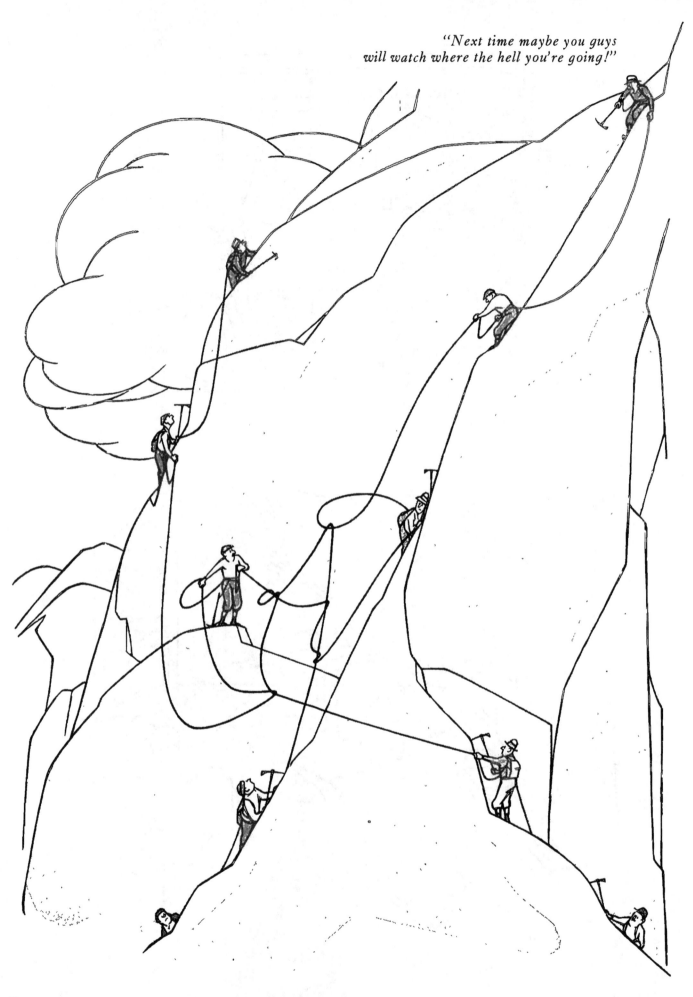

"*Next time maybe you guys will watch where the hell you're going!*"

"And, what's more, just any old bird
won't do. It's got to be a Baltimore oriole."

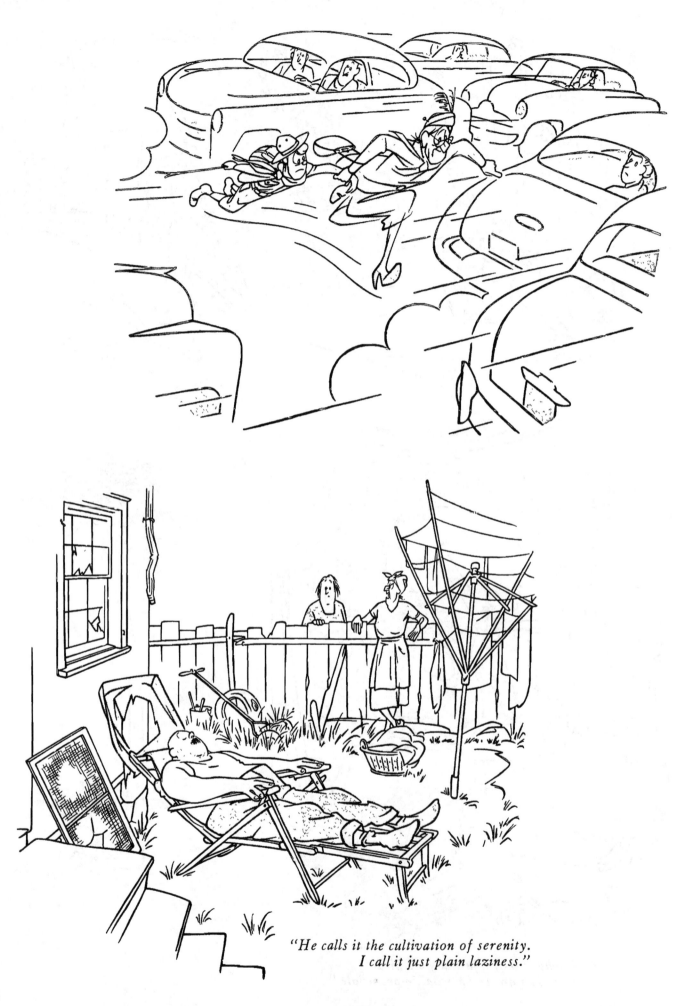

"He calls it the cultivation of serenity.
I call it just plain laziness."

"Hands off that dial!"

"Ride the umpire, folks—1,000 salty taunts,
insults, wisecracks, jeers—only 15 cents!"

"William begat Ichabod, Ichabod begat James,
and James begat Herbie. But in Herbie they've hit a dead end."

"Any minute now we're due for one of
his outbursts of gloomy philosophy."

"Stop hanging around! When
it's ready to be christened I'll tell you."

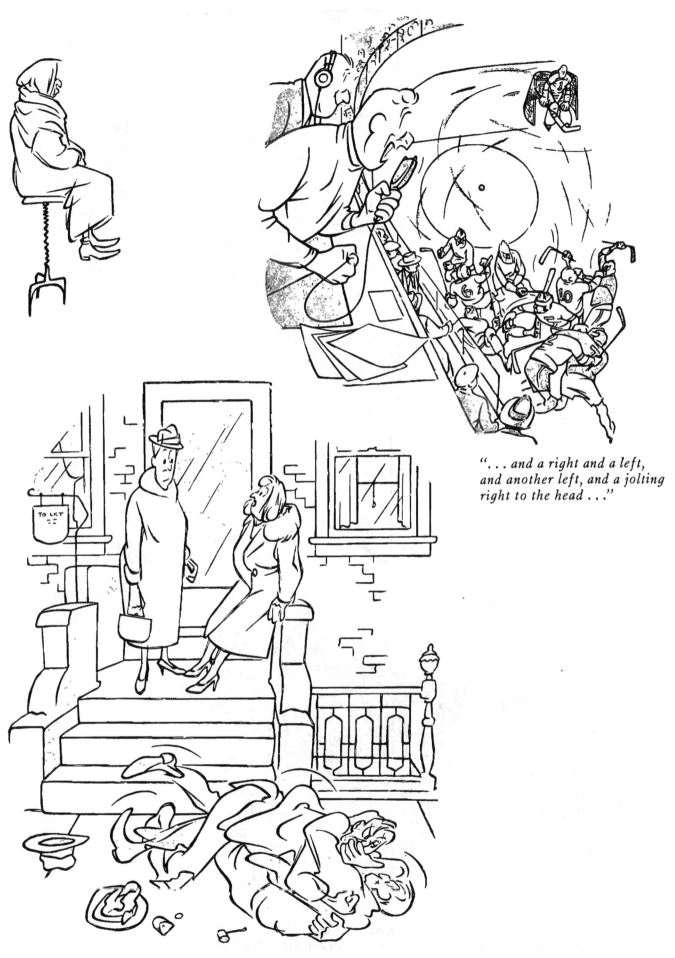

"... and a right and a left, and another left, and a jolting right to the head ..."

"It's over a woman—me."

"How should I know? Maybe it's
National Optometry Week."

"See what I mean? All the time orchids, orchids,
orchids! Do you suppose there could be another Kathleen McCurdy?"

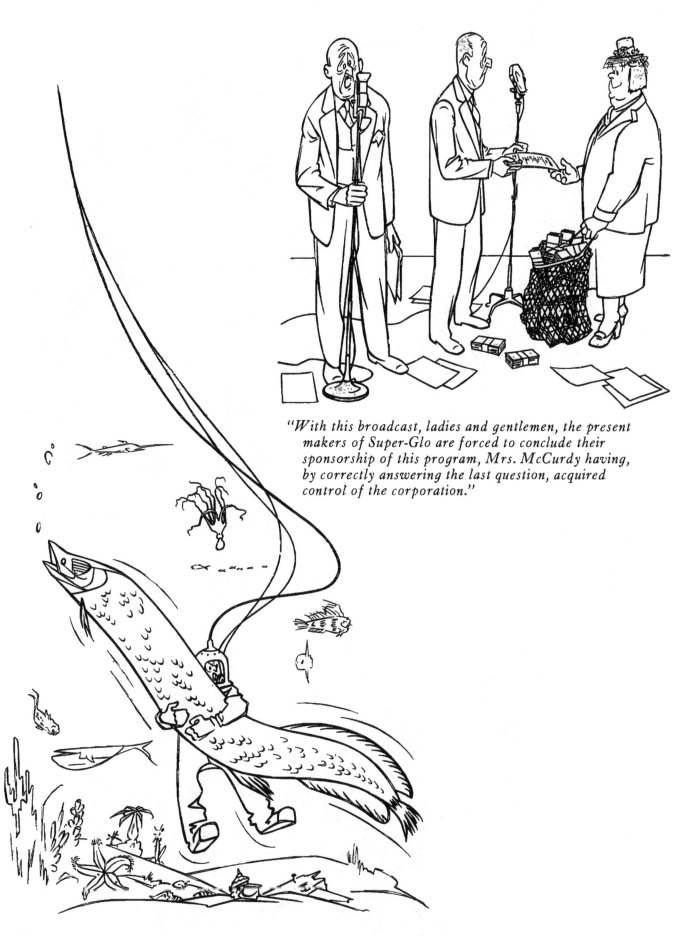

"With this broadcast, ladies and gentlemen, the present
makers of Super-Glo are forced to conclude their
sponsorship of this program, Mrs. McCurdy having,
by correctly answering the last question, acquired
control of the corporation."

"If you were down here, you'd damn well know why I keep saying 'we.'"

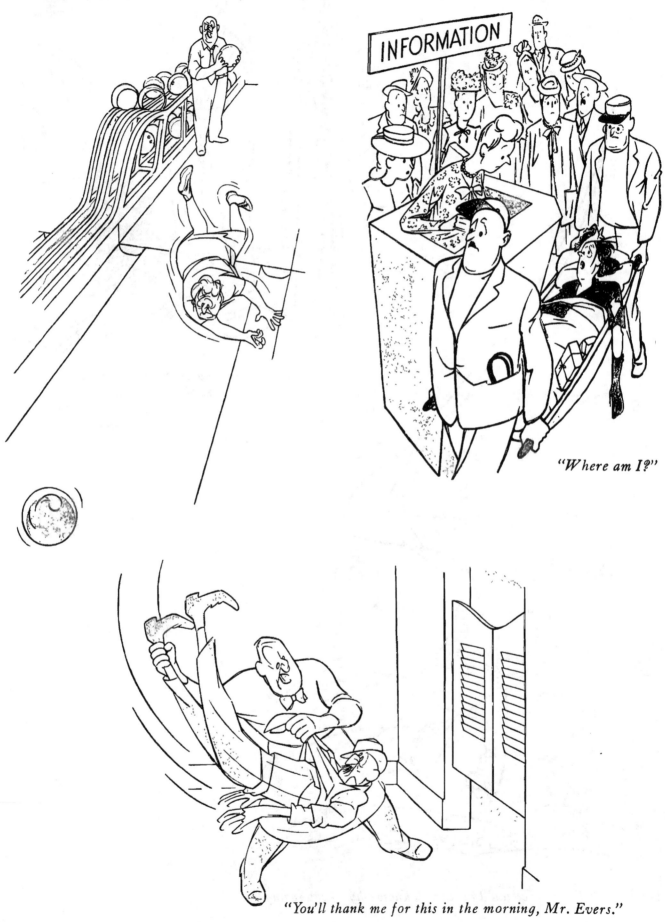

"Watch it, Edith! You're over the foul line again."

"Where am I?"

"You'll thank me for this in the morning, Mr. Evers."

"*For some time now, McCarthy, we haven't been satisfied with your waddle.*"

"*I never saw two fighters more evenly matched.*"

"Forty-five cents a pound—as is."

"You're the first white man to scale this peak. I'm part Indian."

*"At least you have
to give him credit for trying."*

"Now let me take one of you four."

"Congratulations, Madam! You've just acquired
an exquisite example of eighteenth-century Astbury."

"Hmm, elm-tree blight. Can't give you more than twelve dollars for him."

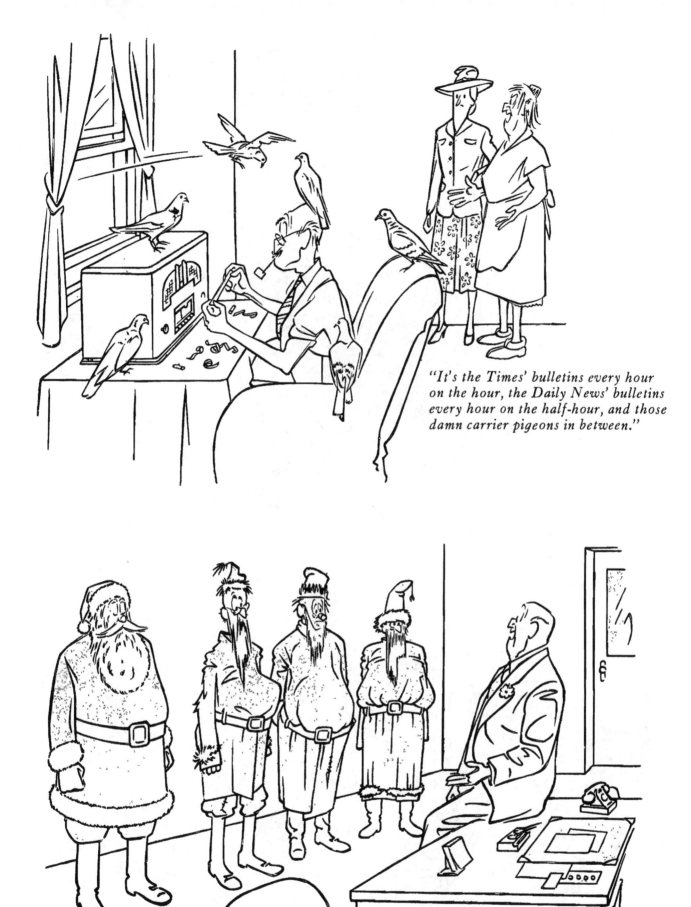

"It's the Times' bulletins every hour on the hour, the Daily News' bulletins every hour on the half-hour, and those damn carrier pigeons in between."

"It all boils down to the question of personal daintiness, men, which Gallagher here has to an unusual degree."

"Say when."

"Objection!"

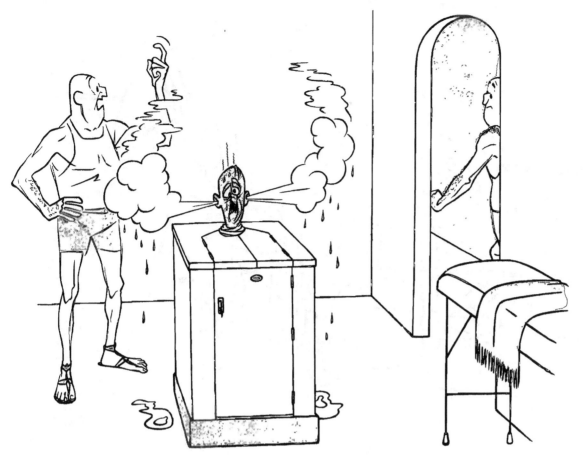

"Say, Jackson, here's something curious."

"To tell you a secret, they're only marked down
to discourage shoplifting. At this price it don't pay to steal them."

"Now get in there and last!"

"Sure there's something you can do. You can lay out the place cards."

"Got any tokens?"

"James J. Harris, attorney at law.
My card, sir, in case you're overtaken."

"In all our married years he's raised his voice
to me only once, and then I think it was because of a low-flying B-29."

"Shouldn't there be bars or a moat or something between us and him?"

"I hope you're a music lover."

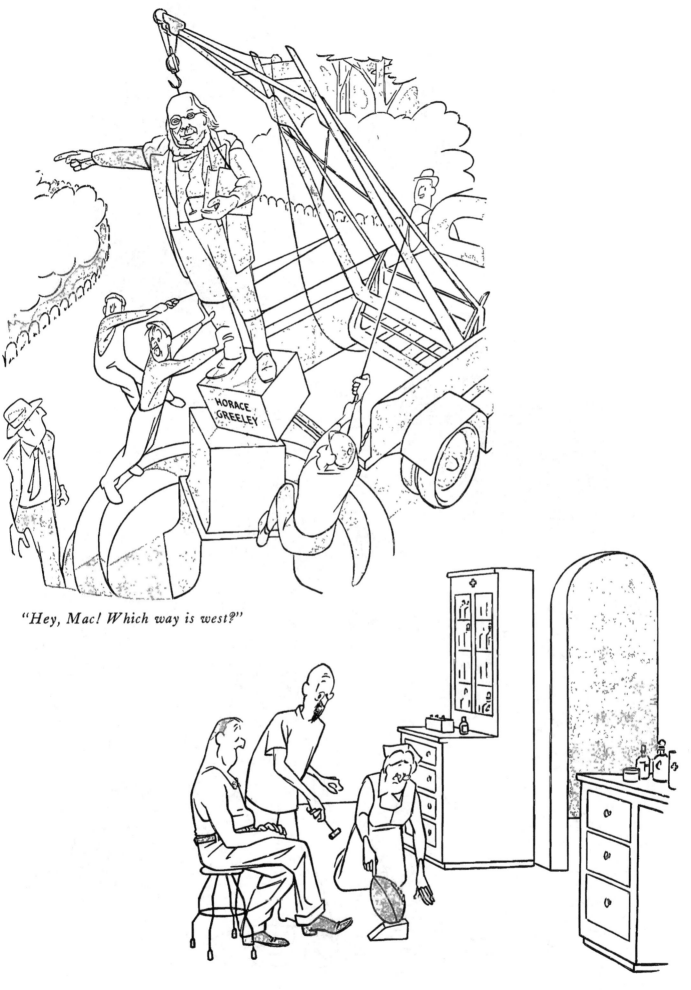

"Hey, Mac! Which way is west?"

"All we can do
is sit tight for a minute
and see what develops."

"Sixty bucks a day this sunshine is costing me, and you have to sit in the shade!"

"Nobody liked anything."

"Madam, I'm from the A.&P.!"

"*That's not necessary here,
Madam. The room clerk will keep it for you.*"

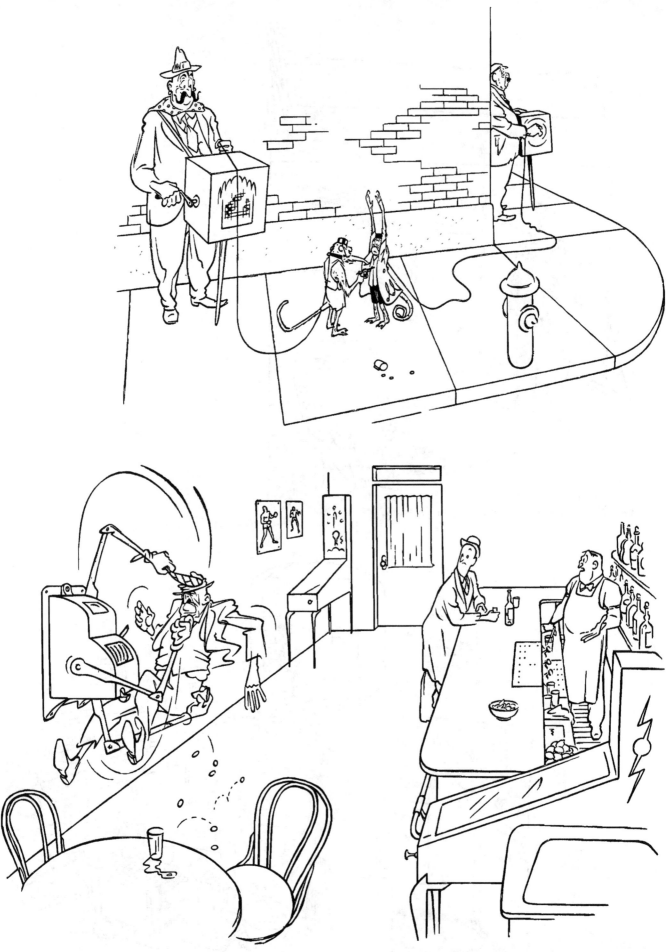

"*The house does wonderful on that one.*"

"Now, this in no way obligates you."

"I did shout for help, but the tide of battle suddenly changed in my favor, thank you."

"...and the balance of my estate I want to put into a trust for the care and maintenance of my most loyal friend and faithful companion, my dog Spot. Now go out and get me a dog with spots."

"Mind removing your hat, sir? This is the Chef's Special."

"Mr. and Mrs. Herman L. Lembaugh of
435 Grand Concourse, the Bronx, offer their only daughter, Ethel, to the winner of a five-lap sprint."

CPSIA information can be obtained
at www.ICGtesting.com
Printed in the USA
LVHW052005041222
734568LV00008B/377